SCHOOL

Why does the wind blow?

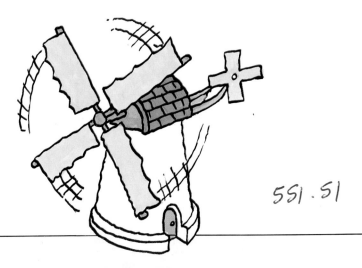

551.51

Written by
Alison Niblo and Hazel Songhurst

Illustrated by Robin Lawrie

Designed by Ross Thomson

Watts

LONDON • NEW YORK • SYDNEY

On a windy day your hair blows about. Washing flaps in the wind. Sometimes the wind whistles down chimneys or howls around the corners of houses.

Try this

Keep a windy weather diary. Hang ribbons or strips of material from a string in the garden. Look at them every day and draw what you see.

No wind: ribbons hang down

Some wind: ribbons blow a little

Windy: ribbons blow about a lot

Very windy: ribbons almost blow away

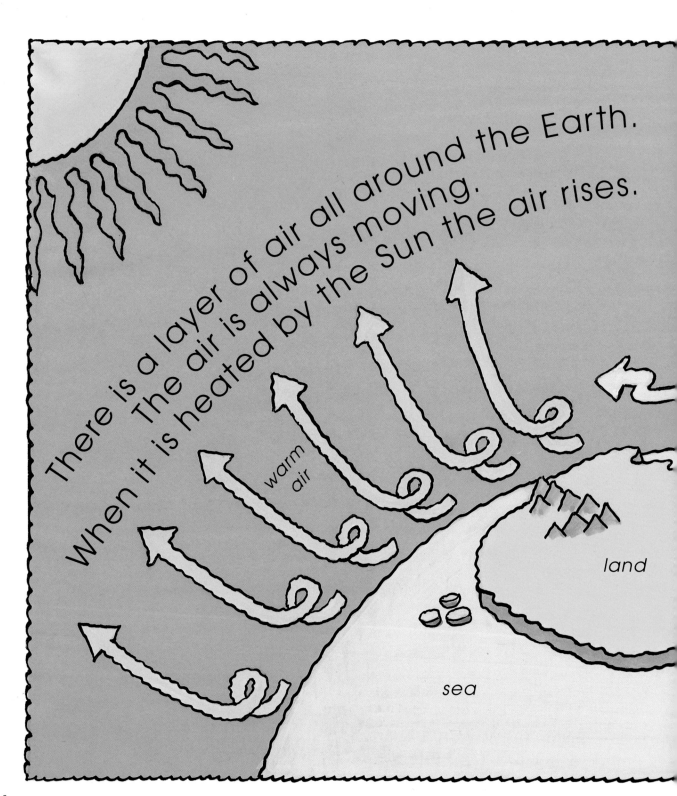

There is a layer of air all around the Earth. The air is always moving. When it is heated by the Sun the air rises.

warm air

land

sea

4

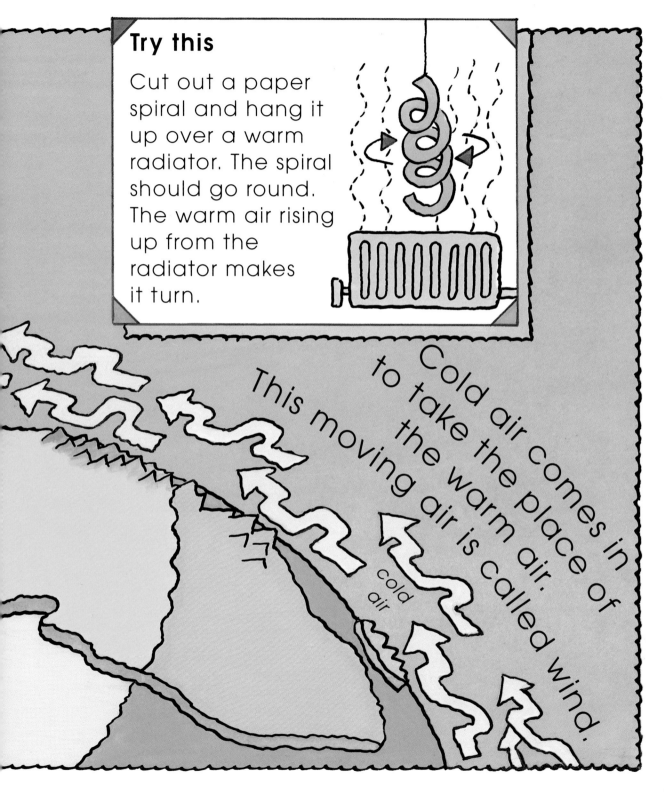

Try this

Cut out a paper spiral and hang it up over a warm radiator. The spiral should go round. The warm air rising up from the radiator makes it turn.

Cold air comes in to take the place of the warm air. This moving air is called wind.

cold air

The wind can be a gentle breeze. But when warm air rises quickly, cold air rushes in to take its place. Then the wind can be a strong gale.

Try this

Put blobs of runny paint on to a piece of paper. Blow gently at them through a drinking straw.

7

In some places it is always windy. At the sea-side, cool sea-breezes blow on to the land. They come in to take the place of the air that is rising from the warm land.

Try this

Make a paper windmill.

1. Fold a square of thin card into a triangle. Fold the triangle in half.

2. Open out the card. Cut along the fold lines to 1 cm from the centre.

3. Bend over four corners into the centre and push through a drawing pin.

Push the pin into a cork. Blow the sails to make them go round.

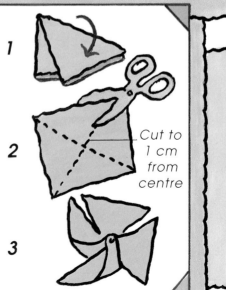

1

2 Cut to 1 cm from centre

3

When wind blows against a hill or cliff it gets pushed upwards. Birds like to hover and soar in the sky on these rising air streams.

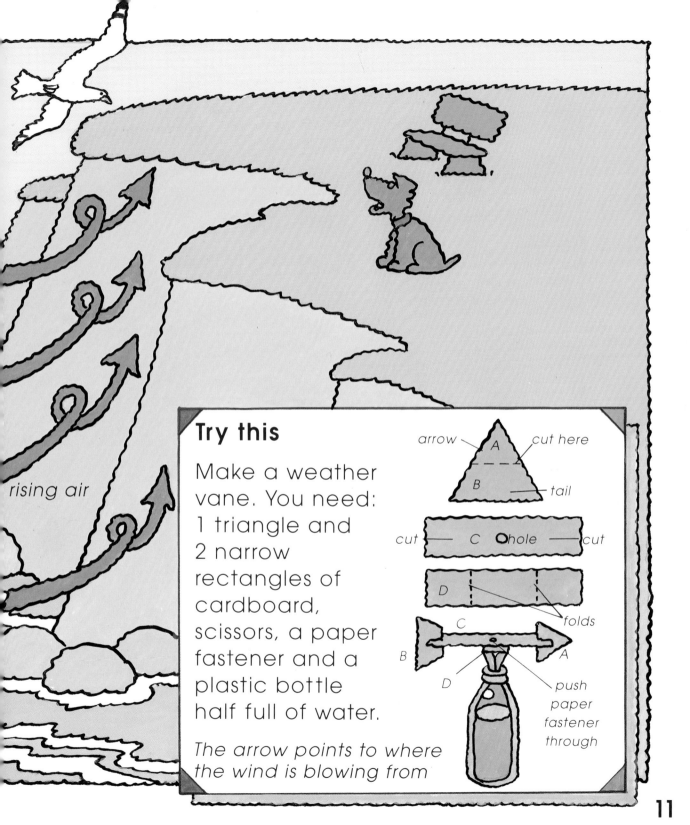

rising air

Try this

Make a weather vane. You need: 1 triangle and 2 narrow rectangles of cardboard, scissors, a paper fastener and a plastic bottle half full of water.

The arrow points to where the wind is blowing from

arrow
A
cut here
B
tail

cut — C ⚫hole — cut

D
folds

C
B
A
D
push paper fastener through

One especially
strong wind is called
a hurricane.
This is a wind which
travels very fast
and causes a lot
of damage.
It can blow over
big trees and even
knock down buildings.

Try this

Make hurricane sounds on a tape recorder. Blow and whistle into the microphone, bang a tray with a spoon, shake dried beans in a tin for rain sounds.

In some parts of the world,
a powerful wind called a
tornado sometimes blows.
A tornado spins around
very fast. It pulls up
heavy objects
into the air.

Try this

Run water into a sink. Pull out the plug and watch the water run away. It makes a spiral cone shape. This is the same shape as a tornado.

In a hot desert, the wind blows dust and sand up from the ground into the air. It makes a huge sandstorm cloud that blows along.

Try this

Draw a desert scene. Spread glue on the sandy areas. Shake over real sand, dried rice or glitter.

For centuries, the wind has been used to blow ships across the sea and to turn the sails of windmills.

Try this

Make a sailing boat. Push a pencil through a square of paper. Use modelling clay to fix the pencil into an empty margarine tub. Put the boat in the bath. Blow into the sail.

Machines can also make wind. Hairdryers blow out warm air to dry your wet hair. Electric fans send out a breeze to cool you down on a hot day.

Try this

Make a fan to keep you cool. Draw a pattern on a sheet of paper. Make a narrow fold down one side. Turn the paper over and fold again. When the whole sheet is folded, hold one end and open out the fan.

The wind can be fun too.
We can fly kites in the wind,
windsurf on the sea, and hang
glide off hills into the air.

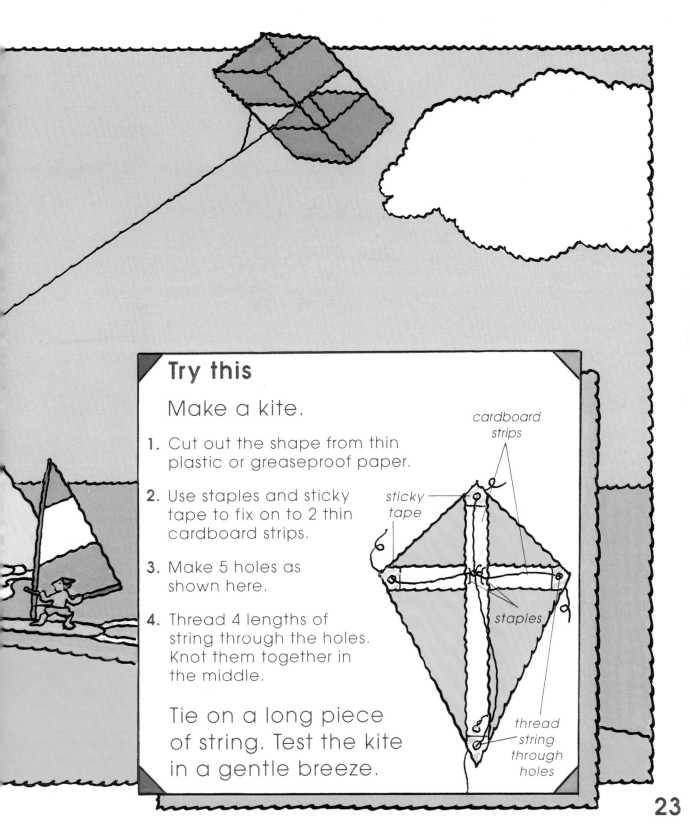

Try this

Make a kite.

1. Cut out the shape from thin plastic or greaseproof paper.

2. Use staples and sticky tape to fix on to 2 thin cardboard strips.

3. Make 5 holes as shown here.

4. Thread 4 lengths of string through the holes. Knot them together in the middle.

Tie on a long piece of string. Test the kite in a gentle breeze.

cardboard strips

sticky tape

staples

thread string through holes

INDEX

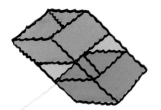

Produced by Zigzag Publishing Ltd,
The Barn, Randolph's Farm, Brighton Road,
Hurstpierpoint, West Sussex BN6 9EL, England

Consultant: Dr Anne Qualter, Centre for
Research in Primary Science and Technology,
Liverpool University

Editors: Janet De Saulles and Hazel Songhurst
Senior Editor: Nicola Wright
Series Concept: Tony Potter

Colour separations: Scan Trans, Singapore
Printer: G. Canale & Co. SpA., Italy

First published in 1993 in the UK by Watts Books
This edition 1995.

Copyright © 1993 Zigzag Pubiishing Ltd

BRITISH LIBRARY CATALOGUING IN PUBLICATION DATA A CIP
catalogue record for this book is available from the
British Library

Dewey Decimal Classification 551.57

ISBN 0 7496 1179 0